# Everything Matters

*A Collection of Poems*

*and*

*the photos which inspired them*

*by*

*Kathleen Kramer*

*For Jack*

*50 years of laughing
with my husband—
better than gold!*

ISBN 978-0-9837768-7-7

Copyright © 2020 by Kathleen Kramer

All rights reserved.

Books are available through the publisher and **amazon.com**, as well as at bookstores in the Ithaca, NY area.

## Credits:

All of the photographs in *Everything Matters* were taken by the author, **Kathleen Kramer,** with these exceptions:

**Author Photo** (pg. v) — by a kind stranger who was visiting Taughannock Falls in Trumansburg, NY, at the same time as Kathy and her husband, Jack.

Grampian Farmhouse, 1949 (pg. 25) — by **Keith Caldwell,** the author's father.

4th of July (pg. 65) — by **Jack Kramer.**

Cover and book design by **E. Nan Edmunds.**

## About the Author

Living in Upstate New York for more than 27 years, Kathleen Kramer and her husband, Jack, have had easy access to the many waterfalls which grace the Finger Lakes area. In this photo, taken at Taughannock Falls on New Year's Day, 2020, Kathy and Jack are continuing their tradition of visiting as many waterfalls as possible on that day. They feel the fact that every drop of water in every waterfall is launching itself into a new adventure seems to fit with this day of beginnings.

Kathy's early years were spent in Pennsylvania's coalmining and farming region, where life was lived in the midst of a large extended family and influenced by the solidity of the earth and the rhythm of seasons. At 19, she left for the city and spent five years working in Washington, DC, for the Department of Defense. There followed a three-year stint in Maine where subsistence farming took her back to the land. New York state was the family's next home and Kathy and Jack reared three sons, Andrew, Ian and Kyle, in Northport, a small historical village on Long Island Sound.

During that time and over a period of 10 years of balancing classes, family and work, Kathy earned a BA at Empire State College and an MLS at Long Island University. Now, following retirement from the Boyce Thompson Institute at Cornell, she continues to write poetry and plays, while also supporting, in various roles, The Church of the Epiphany in Trumansburg. This book is her third full-length collection, preceded by *Planting Wild Grapes* in 2016 and *Boiled Potato Blues* in 2011.

## Author's Note

The title of this collection was given to me more than thirty years ago. I was sitting near the harbor in Northport, NY, watching the masts of moored sailboats swaying like metronomes; the gulls wheeling, carrying the afternoon light on their backs. And I was thinking about writing and the way that a piece that felt authentic and true seemed to come from me, but from something beyond me, as well.

Suddenly, there was a profound feeling of being connected with that "something beyond," and a thought was given into my heart: *Everything Matters… And Nothing Matters.*

I was stunned and moved. And, later when I shared this with a few friends, several likened it to a Koan in the Zen Buddhist tradition. And, indeed, as I've contemplated it over the years, it does challenge logical thinking and calls for a deeper reality, better understood by intuition and the spirit.

For a long time, I didn't know what to do with this. But it kept coming onto my "radar," so to speak, and finally, it has found some expression in this collection, with the first phrase, Everything Matters, becoming its title.

Although these photographs, these poems, have been part of the journey, I had no plan in mind when I took the photos. If I saw something that caught me—a pattern of shadows on the post office steps, a narrow walkway with a lock on its gate, a tiny snowman—I didn't stop to think; I just took the photo and felt pleased and fed.

Then later—hours, weeks, even years later—the photographs and I—and something beyond?—spoke in these poems.

For me, they are both praise and process, full with thanksgiving and joy, as well as the acceptance of impermanence.

Everything changes. Everything passes. For these reasons, and for the very fact of existence, everything matters.

—Kathleen Kramer

# Acknowledgements

The author gratefully acknowledges The Healing Muse for its publication of "Every Other Thing."

In addition, "October" and "To a Geranium" were previously published in *Planting Wild Grapes*, a collection of poems by the author.

Sincere appreciation to my poetry group, The High Noon Poets, for their expert and sensitive critiques of nearly every poem in this collection. Deepest gratitude to Nan Edmunds for her technical skills and her fine sense of aesthetics in creating the design and layout of *Everything Matters*. Her input on editorial decisions was invaluable. And, as always, thank you to my husband, Jack, for being the first to read and offer his insightful thoughts on each poem, and for his unfailing support and encouragement for the entire 50 years of our marriage.

# *Foreword*

In her newest volume of poems and accompanying photographs, **Kathleen Kramer** has given both poets and photographers and their fellow travelers a great gift. Poets will find here yet again her inimitable gifts of patient attending to what wants to be revealed along with the rigorous discipline of finding just the needed words to sing her subjects into being on the page.

Photographers will discover that her photographs also sing when we forego the all too common descriptors of our efforts as "snapshots" or "captures." With her gentle and loving attention to each of these beautiful images, Kramer has taken us further into her own unique spiritual language of glory and praise. Having read and re-read this volume with the slowness needed, we might finally come to see poem and image as together doing what all classic religious Icons do: open our hearts to the silent center, where we can be still and lovingly know another being, even as we in turn are known and loved.

                    The Rev. Dr. Clark R. West, Pastor,
                    St. Philip's Episcopal Church, Akron, Ohio

## Contents

Still Life . . . . . . . . . . . . . . . . . . . . . . . . . . . . . . . . 13

Small Things . . . . . . . . . . . . . . . . . . . . . . . . . . . . .15

To a Geranium . . . . . . . . . . . . . . . . . . . . . . . . . . .17

Bilger's Rocks . . . . . . . . . . . . . . . . . . . . . . . . . . . 19

Meditation on a Goldfish . . . . . . . . . . . . . . . . . . 21

Lines . . . . . . . . . . . . . . . . . . . . . . . . . . . . . . . . . 23

Grampian Farmhouse, 1949 . . . . . . . . . . . . . . . .25

I am too full to write a proper poem . . . . . . . . . . 27

Dump Truck . . . . . . . . . . . . . . . . . . . . . . . . . . 29

Silver Haired Daddy . . . . . . . . . . . . . . . . . . . . . 30

Not So Long Ago . . . . . . . . . . . . . . . . . . . . . . .33

October . . . . . . . . . . . . . . . . . . . . . . . . . . . . . .35

Entertaining St. Paul . . . . . . . . . . . . . . . . . . . . . 37

Visiting Cercis Canadensis . . . . . . . . . . . . . . . . . 39

Super 8 . . . . . . . . . . . . . . . . . . . . . . . . . . . . . . 41

From a Teenage Son . . . . . . . . . . . . . . . . . . . . . 43

Moth . . . . . . . . . . . . . . . . . . . . . . . . . . . . . . . 45

Door . . . . . . . . . . . . . . . . . . . . . . . . . . . . . . . 47

The poet lies on her back in the graveyard . . . . . . . . 49

two beloved dogs sleep . . . . . . . . . . . . . . . . . . . . . 51

It's been said many times— . . . . . . . . . . . . . . . . . 53

Impressions . . . . . . . . . . . . . . . . . . . . . . . . . . . . . 55

At the Park, the Day Before Christmas . . . . . . . . . . 57

a tiny boy . . . . . . . . . . . . . . . . . . . . . . . . . . . . . . 59

fifty years ago . . . . . . . . . . . . . . . . . . . . . . . 61

Snail, On Being a Snail . . . . . . . . . . . . . . . . . . . . 63

4th of July— . . . . . . . . . . . . . . . . . . . . . . . . . . . 65

Safe and Sorry . . . . . . . . . . . . . . . . . . . . . . . . . . 67

Passage . . . . . . . . . . . . . . . . . . . . . . . . . . . . . . . 69

Evening Has a Way . . . . . . . . . . . . . . . . . . . . . . 71

Graduation . . . . . . . . . . . . . . . . . . . . . . . . . . . . 73

I am a part-time sailor now
  and my name changes in every port . . . . . . . . . . . 75

As this night turns over . . . . . . . . . . . . . . . . . . . 77

wanting nothing . . . . . . . . . . . . . . . . . . . . . . . . 79

Everything Matters . . . . . . . . . . . . . . . . . . . . . 80

Walk with me . . . . . . . . . . . . . . . . . . . . . . . . . . 83

Every Other Thing . . . . . . . . . . . . . . . . . . . . . . 85

# Still Life

It seems that a blue bowl holding a smooth
white egg and piece of sky must have meaning,

perhaps something profound. But for years,
this picture has been silent, its images inscrutable,

or so full of possibilities as to overwhelm.
Finally, today, I surrendered, and simply gazed

at the shapes, the curves, the colors—
the way they echo each other.

It was only then that the bowl, the egg, the sky
spoke with one voice.

*We simply are.*
                     *And we please you.*

I know they spoke truth. And although the egg—
that particular egg—is gone, I still have the bowl.

And if the bowl should break,
I'll have the sky.

## *Small Things*

These days, it's the small things—
like this little snowman—
that give delight to darkness.

We almost missed him, sitting quietly
as he was, on a bench outside
the doctor's office.

But his bright baby-carrot nose
caught us. Then the button eyes and
his cap of leaf and twig.

He sat there, watching all who passed
with eyes sober & kind. And we thought
of the one who made him—

how gloves were shucked off,
stuffed in a jacket pocket
so that fingers, quickly stiffening,

could wrap the blue tie, place the greens
at his base—in tribute to Christmas,
perhaps. We hope the creator knows

how much this little being has added,
temporary and ephemeral though
he may be, just by the fact that he is.

# To a Geranium

I don't blame you. It's me has kept you
in that coffee mug. Gangly and gawky,
you must be strangling on your roots.

But you were a gift—Mother's Day
years and years ago—from a young son
with empty pockets, and my heart wants you

to stay where you were planted. You stand
on the sill above the sink, mere inches from
the faucet. Still I often fail to give you water

until I see one of your leaves has dropped,
dry and disconsolate. Yet this morning,
I came into the kitchen and there,

resting against the window like the head
of a weary traveler on a bus, was a bloom
so red, it sang.

*For Ian*

## Bilger's Rocks

It's the boulder
at the bottom
that bears the weight.
See how it leans, partly
buried in the yielding ground.


Listen now and
you'll hear it groan,
but only if you know
the sound of one whose
shoulders are broad and strong
                and always there.


**Note:** Bilger's Rocks is a sandstone outcropping near the Susquehanna River in Western PA. It is 316-320 million years old and predates the breakup of the ancient supercontinent, Pangaea.

## Meditation on a Goldfish

From time to time I must go apart
where I am sheltered
   from duty
      from pleasantries
         …even love

I must go where all is silence
where the only things to see
   are flecks of dust floating and
      shafts of light from a source
         beyond sight

I must stay there until I hear only
heart thud
   blood surge
      and *being* takes the place
         of striving to be

# Lines

*For my mother*

On paper torn from a tablet
and marked with lines as faint
and blue as the veins in her hand
she writes to me

646 miles away I wait
for the mail to come
hold the envelope in cold fingers
picture her

climbing the post office steps
pushing open the heavy door
dropping her letter
through the slot

marked *OUT OF TOWN*
I thought all I needed was
to get away—and it was
But when she wrote

of shelling peas on the porch
with Aunt Honey or taking
my little brothers to the fair
I thought all I needed was
          to go home

# Grampian Farmhouse, 1949

An old house, yes, unpainted and curtainless,
it seems to speak of certain decline, but

the man who stands on the hill pointing
his camera sees the girl on the porch,

proud in her Dale Evans vest, dungarees
rolled and cuffed with enough room to grow

and the woman on the bench, thick auburn hair
to her shoulders, their baby, named for him,

at her knee, and the black and white cat
called Tom rubbing against her ankles while

they all wait for the chicken dinner, roasting
in the coal stove in the kitchen, and for him

to finish the picture and wave as he runs,
headlong, down the weedy hill.

# *I am too full to write a proper poem*

too brimmed
with dear old men
teetering
at the edge
of their lives

to know
if this is where
the stanza break
should be
here just before

new babies
crying for the breast
smiling
at shadows
on the blinds or

here with weddings
of pale gray and ivory
or with ministers who
wear red shirts and
clown noses

it seems appropriate
to break before
old friends
from fifty years past
dancing the twist

and here
where I tell about
cousins
dishing potato salad
onto paper plates

and my brother
with fading eyes
who may be able
to drive again
after this final break

God willing.

# Dump Truck

*For my father, at 99*

With no load to carry
why go on? An empty bed
does nothing but bang and boom
hollowly over the rough road.

Rust eats at the edges and who knows
what the undercarriage is like.
Maybe it's time to park in an empty lot,
hang up the keys and let weeds grow,
rank, through the floorboards.

But The Driver can still hoist himself
into the cab. He can still roll down
the window, rest an elbow in the sun,
and dream into the big rearview mirror.

# *Silver Haired Daddy*

In dress blues, his sailor cap
at a jaunty angle, the young man
smiles. He gazes at the old man
in the wheel chair, gazing back.

Their eyes meet and each recognizes
the other across the span
of a continent, an ocean, and
seventy-five years.

They share the loneliness
of a narrow bunk, joy of a letter
from home, the wait at a pay phone
to call the young wife left behind.

The vision of torpedoes
slashing through raging waves,
Japanese Zeros diving from the sky,
rescued POWs, ragged and thin.

Then flashing between them like a deck
of cards, rapidly shuffled and redealt,
the homecoming, the little house,
five children, the loss of one.

Picking blackberries, huckleberries,
teaching the kids to skip stones, play
Crokinole, decorate the Christmas tree
cut from plantings at the strip mines.

The fragrance of fallen leaves,
coal smoke, fresh-baked johnnycake,
Trailing-Arbutus on the bank
of the Susquehanna.

And the voices—whispering love
and prayers, weeping and laughing,
raised in anger, lifted in song—
*Silver Haired Daddy, Amazing Grace.*

> Silver Haired Daddy *was written in 1931 by Gene Autry and Jimmy Long and became Autry's first hit song. It was later recorded by the Everly Brothers, Simon & Garfunkel, and others.*

# Not So Long Ago

There was music here. A piano,
probably in need of tuning, and
voices rolling out the old hymns—
*Rock of ages, cleft for me* and
*Precious Lord, take my hand.*
There were new babies to bless,
brides and grooms, resplendent
and trembling. Mourners leaned on
each other's shoulders, sharing tears.

Not so long ago, there were picnic suppers
on the grounds—a hayfield freshly mown
to make a place for sawhorse tables
draped with wind-sweetened sheets and
laden with bowls of potato salad,
baked beans bubbling in their crocks,
sliced ham, soft rolls piled like pillows.
And the gentle joke about who brought
the deviled eggs, who brought the angel food.

# *October*

Forty years ago, I fell in love
with yellow—wake-me-up,
eyes-open, heart-lift yellow.

*Egg-yolk lemon-butter primrose
dandelion bumble-bee goldfinch
Easter-chick blonde-baby yellow.*

Forty years ago, my mother,
blindness fast encroaching, told me—
*It's the only color I still see.*

Now, here, under this canopy
of maples, the very air is yellow.
I listen for that tiny sound

each leaf makes when it lets go
the twig, hold my breath
lest one leaf fall too soon.

# Entertaining St. Paul

*For Gillian*

*Come and sit,* I say.
The air is mild and the sky
is closing its eye on the day.
*May I bring you a drink?*

But what would he like, I wonder.
Perhaps water—Adam's ale,
as it's called. Or wine, pressed
from wild grapes and blessed.

I have only this Merlot
and I apologize as I pour.
He is gracious, accepting
the glass with a weary smile.

He's been everywhere and now
he's here. So many questions
I have…. What really happened
on the road to Damascus?

What was the thorn that plagued him
all his life? But I see his shoulders
slump. His sandals are scuffed
and covered with dust.

So I say nothing. Side by side
we gaze into the darkening valley,
listen to the flutter of tiny wings
as a moth circles the light,
        softly beating, beating.

# Visiting Cercis Canadensis

# Visiting Cercis Canadensis

On Tuesday I took these photos—
Redbuds in the ecstasy of May.

As hungry for spring as a wakened bear,
I clicked away, claiming this beauty for myself—

compensation for an epic winter,
a charm calling forth my youthful soul.

On Wednesday I went to visit my Redbuds
again, but they were not alone. Instead,

a young woman was there, standing
exactly where I had stood, clicking away

from the same angles I had used.
Her camera was much fancier than mine.

Striving for generosity of spirit, a shared love
of beauty, I smiled at her. She didn't return

my smile, probably thinking these Redbuds
are *hers* now.

# Super 8

He pulled in here within sight
of the Interstate at one this morning,
parked his rig and fell into bed, a luxury

he allows himself every three days.
If you ask him what he does, he'll say
in the lingo of the road, *I drive truck.*

The breakfast here's not bad. They
even have one of those waffle-makers,
but he opts for eggs—yellow disks of

sponge rubber—but hell, they're protein.
His wife back in Illinois would be proud.
He'll call her before he hits the road.

*Clear to partly cloudy, ten percent chance
of rain.* Hope it holds. He remembers
his last run through West Virginia, grinding

up those mountains in a storm, toting a load
of heavy equipment, wipers keeping time
with Merle Haggard, Del McCoury.

*Them boys is good company, but they don't
listen much.* Talking to himself scares him,
though, so between songs, there's a lot of quiet

in his cab. He thinks about the loneliness
from time to time, but figures when you come
right down to it, everyone's alone on the inside.

# From a Teenage Son

*for Kyle*

Even in the dark, he can see
        the pale tulip, its soft chalice
swaying in a breeze from The Sound.

Small-town gardens, neatly-bordered,
        offer a wealth of flowers. He tiptoes
from one to another, picks a white one

here, yellow there, never taking more
        than two from any garden. Finally,
having amassed a vast armful,

he ventures home, places them
        in a clear glass vase, and leaves them
on the dining room table for me
        to find on Mother's Day morning.

# Moth

Two days after Annie died
the moth came to my window

Autumn chill had stiffened
its wings but the soft body
still pulsed with life

My finger on the glass
created a halo and I wondered—

Can she feel the warmth
on her side of the pane
that divides us

# Door

> *Either you will go through this door*
> *or you will not go through—*
> Adrienne Rich

Simple on the face of it—
either I see you here
   on this side

or I don't
and know
   you're on the other

know you've crossed
   a threshold and
nothing is the same

All this implies ease
   free will

But what of compulsion
   fear  passion  time

or some push
   some pull
we know only dimly

And dare we speak
   of destiny
in this equation

Finally though
   there is memory
which opens all doors

leaves them standing
   wide

so everything becomes now
   becomes here

# *The poet lies on her back in the graveyard*

cushioned by grass    cooled by shade
intending to contemplate deeply the meaning
of this place    beyond the down-to-earth
reasons for its being

to discern the mystery it may hold
with its burden of bodies    souls
set free or still held captive by unfinished
business    work undone

she closes her eyes to better feel
if there is life here other than hers
and that of the cardinal declaring himself
from the old maple

she tries to get a sense of the person
lying beneath her    dust and maybe
a few bones in a shape approximating
her own

so little separates them    dirt    roots
the lid of a box and of course time
which stopped in this world for
Hannah Nobles on April 7 1894

were the crocuses blooming
the poet wonders and hopes they were
there in Hannah's dooryard
yellow and purple pushing through
the last snow

two beloved dogs sleep
beneath the snow
mother moon keeps watch

# It's been said many times—

*A Cathedral…*
    where shadow and light
    weave lamentation and praise

Or the pipes of a grand organ
    where the wind plays
    its sacred hymn

But what of those fallen
    prostrate and silent
    on the forest floor

What of redemption
    resurrection
    rebirth

Consider rain and snow
    beetle and mouse
    ceaseless time and grace

until finally they become
    good ground where
    seeds burst and reach

If transformation
    takes many years
    is it any less a miracle

# *Impressions*

In the throes of a snowy winter, a paralysis
of sorts may claim our souls. Numbing cold
can kill hopes, early dark shroud memories.
And we spend truncated days treading,
retreading, the same aimless tracks.

It's possible, I know, for a whole life
to be winter-bound, where a playground
of the past recedes too far to be recalled
and the colors of a future are too faint
to be found.

But look. The snow is shallow, easy prey
for a weak sun, and the earth will continue
its elliptical path until all children past,
all children future, meet at the tall slide,
taking turns, as they've been taught.

# At the Park, the Day Before Christmas

This is the picture I was taking when
I heard the humming. Coming from
behind me, a voice sweet and soft—

*Silent night, holy night*
*all is calm, all is bright*

Before I turned, I knew the song
was for her—the self, remembering.
But I needed to see her, the young woman—

slim and clad in a dark coat,
hood framing fair hair, quiet face.
She saw me seeing her and spoke,

*How are you?*
My answer surprised me.
*I'm wonderful.*
We shook hands—*Merry Christmas.*
Then, *I'm Kathy.*
*Jan,* she smiled.
*Thank you for this moment,* I said.
*You're welcome.*
And she walked on.

I faced again the trees, yearning upward
on the hillside, and I wept
for all my Christmases.

And for this Christmas,
    come just now.

a tiny boy
from a big city—
first snow, first sled

Fifty years ago
before everything changed
he nestled warm
in the curve of my arm
and pretended to read

    *I think I can!*
    *I think I can!*

    … And he could

*For Andrew*

## Snail, On Being a Snail

It takes me an hour to go twelve inches
over the rough boards of this deck.

Moving this slowly, I feel every splinter,
every speck, under my soft, undulating foot.

The weight of my spiral shell torques me
to the left and I thank the creator for

having the wisdom to make me spineless,
and for imbuing me with endless patience—

so unlike the poor being looming above me,
rubbing her back, peering at her watch and

groaning as she hitches her little garden stool
to the next plant awaiting her trowel.

4th of July—
sparklers sparkled longer
when I was a girl

# *Safe and Sorry*

It is a day of endings, signaled by
the feathered flags of sumac turning red
and starlings flocking in the stubbled fields.

It is a day to think of things left undone,
of gently accepting old regrets, naming
them so as to let them go, like

never diving from the high board,
preferring instead the cannonball with
nose pinched between cold fingers.

Or refusing a glider ride, telling myself
its cabin would be too confining.
And standing on the sidelines at the rink,

or huddled by the fire at the ski lodge, citing
weak and wobbly ankles. Fear's the culprit,
of course. And unlike the grasshopper,

I could always jump
backwards from the edge.

# Passage

I walk through many gates.
Some—silent on their hinges—
swing closed, then open again,
smoothly, at the touch of my finger,
and I go back the way I have come.

But some clang shut behind me
and when I turn at the sound,
the hand of circumstance, or time,
wraps a chain, snaps a lock.

There is no key, I know, so the only way
is forward and narrow, over boards rough
with splinters, to the end where
a bright fog obscures a fragile stair.

# Evening Has a Way

*for Jack on our 48th anniversary*

We share a love
of black & white
it gives the eye a rest
from the barrage of color

allows us to see
in silhouette
shape and form
light and line

oh there was color
in our lives
sometimes riotous
as fireworks

sometimes quiet
as a sleeping baby
swaddled
in blue

but evening
has a way
of muting the intense
until we see

ripples
and sheen
grace of willow
stillness of gulls

# *Graduation*

*For my granddaughter*

These waters have been plied before.
Countless young women of countless
generations have launched into these waves,

some sailing with the wind, a clear view of
the horizon; some, like me all those years ago,
against the wind, distance shrouded in fog.

Across the widening span of time,
I no longer have instruments to read her.
So I write a letter to this young woman

of my heart, fearful that my words may seem
an ancient chart, outdated. Or an anchor,
mooring her in a harbor outgrown.

But I am journeying, too. And like hers, my sea
is new to me, fraught with cross currents,
hidden shoals. So I pick up my pen and forge

ahead with words like respect, honesty, kindness,
integrity, forgiveness, guts—willing them
to be channel markers for us both.

## *I am a part-time sailor now and my name changes in every port*

In the pre-dawn darkness
if your waking heart said these words
what would you make of it

If you've netted as many years as I have
you would understand
being a part-time sailor—

how one moves more slowly through time
plans only a single thing for this day
or maybe nothing

no longer sees a blank square
on the calendar as bleak and
needing to be filled

But could you imagine your name
changing again and again
who you are dependent on where you are

I lack the art to decipher this part
and I must trust that the port which calls me
will be a worthy namesake

So I weigh anchor and boldly say
*God does not leave us rudderless*
*Let strong winds come*

As this night turns over
my life turns, too, leaving
behind seventy-seven years—

rich and tangled with vines
spangled with flowers,
studded with thorns.

The moment trembles there,
uncertain in the darkened room.
It's a long and a short time

till 12:02. Then 12:03.
(At my age, 12 to 28 breaths
for each minute, they say.)

I resist counting. Instead, I taste
the air, spiced with autumn,
flowing in, flowing out.

wanting nothing
gives me
everything

## Everything Matters

Driving home from the ice cream shop
this summer evening, we glimpse
in the rearview mirror the colors
just beginning to bloom on the horizon.

We turn around (of course we do!) and park
at the crest of the hill in a driveway
marked with a stack of rocks—a cairn,
of sorts, meant to say, *This is the place…*

This is the place to see the life of a sunset
as it unfurls and flings itself across the sky,
timid at first, then bold and glorious. I take
many pictures. This is but one. And then

it is time to stop. Now there will be
no camera between our eyes and the sunset,
no talk between us and the solitary
cricket we hear in the tall grass.

When the sunset finally dies and the cricket
falls silent, we turn again and continue
the drive home—past fields carpeted with
curing hay, past the old barn, weathered

and weakened by the years, past the billboard
that urges, *Repent!*, past the road that leads
to Camilla's home, where she'd spent her last
moments enfolded in the arms of friends.

In our driveway, by the light from the porch,
I see on your shirt one chocolate sprinkle
from your ice cream cone. I touch it with my
fingertip, place its sweetness on my tongue.

# *Walk with me*

There is a place where the clouds float
    breathless    above the ground
where the horizon calls    and the light beyond

There is a road offering itself
    and a wind    bearing the fragrance
of earth warming from winter    but slowly

Walk with me

Walk with me past fence posts
    past telephone poles    slightly leaning
and the three bare trees    Walk with me

and I may not be afraid
    and I may    with ease
        reach the end

# *Every Other Thing*

Even this scarf, gauzy and light
at my throat, feels tight.

Also my waistband, though
the button's undone.

In my mind I see the river
and on the bank, my scarf,

these trousers, and beside them,
Every Other Thing That Binds.

I'm in the water now, sinking
beneath the surface until

greenness closes over me.
My hair streams in the current.

I breathe without thought
as in a dream. Below me

lie the rocks of ages past, inert,
harmless. Above me floats

Every Other Thing That Binds,
passing gently now from view.

www.ingramcontent.com/pod-product-compliance
Lightning Source LLC
Chambersburg PA
CBHW050815090426
42736CB00021B/3466